All Kinds of MAPS

by Susan Ahmadi Hansen

PEBBLE
a capstone imprint

Published by Pebble, an imprint of Capstone
1710 Roe Crest Drive, North Mankato, Minnesota 56003
capstonepub.com

Copyright © 2023 by Capstone. All rights reserved. No part of this publication may be reproduced in whole or in part, or stored in a retrieval system, or transmitted in any form or by any means, electronic, mechanical, photocopying, recording, or otherwise, without written permission of the publisher.

Library of Congress Cataloging-in-Publication Data
Names: Hansen, Susan Ahmadi, author.
Title: All kinds of maps / by Susan Ahmadi Hansen.
Description: North Mankato, Minnesota : Pebble, 2023. | Series: On the map | Includes bibliographical references and index. | Audience: Ages 5-8 | Audience: Grades K-1 |
Summary: "Which highways pass through Wyoming? How much rain did New Orleans get yesterday? How many people live in Texas? Learn about different kinds of maps and how we use them to understand the places and people around us. This first introduction to types of maps will help kids build visual literacy skills and navigate their world"-- Provided by publisher.
Identifiers: LCCN 2022001088 (print) | LCCN 2022001089 (ebook) |
  ISBN 9781666349641 (hardcover) | ISBN 9781666349689 (paperback) |
  ISBN 9781666349726 (pdf) | ISBN 9781666349801 (kindle edition)
Subjects: LCSH: Maps--Juvenile literature. | Map reading--Juvenile literature.
Classification: LCC GA105.6 .H359 2023 (print) | LCC GA105.6 (ebook) | DDC 912.01/4--dc23/eng20220711
LC record available at https://lccn.loc.gov/2022001088
LC ebook record available at https://lccn.loc.gov/2022001089

Editorial Credits
Editor: Ericka Smith; Designer: Tracy Davies;
Media Researcher: Svetlana Zhurkin; Production Specialist: Katy LaVigne

Image Credits
Capstone: Maps.com, 12, 16; Getty Images: shoo_arts, 21, XiXinXing, 18; NOAA: Climate.gov/NDMC, 17; Shutterstock: airdone, 13, ekler, 11, FiledIMAGE, 6, Fourleaflover (map background), cover (right), 1, Hluboki (road), cover (left), Hurst Photo, 19, Ilya Kalinin (doodles), cover (right), Inu, 14, Keangs Seksan (globe), cover (top), Marian Salabai (map), cover (bottom), melissamn, 8, michaeljung, 7, Rawpixel, 5, Serban Bogdan, 9; XNR Productions: 15

All internet sites appearing in back matter were available and accurate when this book was sent to press.

TABLE OF CONTENTS

Why Do We Use Maps?................................4

Paper Maps, Digital Maps, and Globes 6

Physical Maps 8

Political Maps 10

Road Maps.. 12

Other Types of Maps 14

Using Maps 18

    Learning from Maps...................... 20

    Glossary 22

    Read More 23

    Internet Sites 23

    Index... 24

    About the Author 24

Words in **bold** are in the glossary.

Why Do We Use Maps?

Maps aren't just pictures of places. They teach us about places. A map might show where a country is. Or it could show what the land looks like.

There are many kinds of maps. They help us understand a lot about our world.

Paper Maps, Digital Maps, and Globes

Most maps are paper maps. They are easy to take with you. **Digital** maps are on computers and phones. You can find places quickly.

A **globe** is a map of Earth. It is drawn on a **sphere**. A sphere is round, like Earth. So a globe shows our planet's shape well. But it can't show many details.

Physical Maps

A physical map shows natural **features**. It can show mountains and valleys. It can also show rivers, lakes, and oceans.

North America

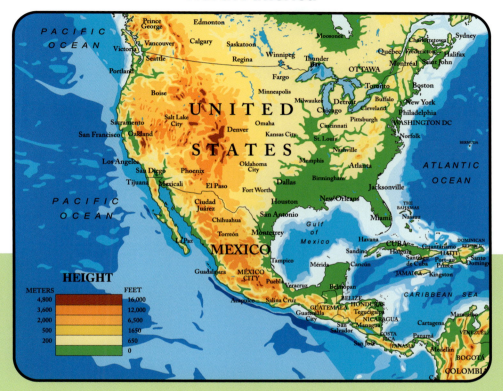

Colors can show how high a place is. Mountains are often darker colors. Deserts are often lighter colors. The **key** helps you understand how high different areas are.

Political Maps

A political map shows the borders of places like states and countries. Black lines usually show borders.

Political maps can also show important places like **capitals** and big cities. Circles usually show important cities. Stars usually show capitals.

Road Maps

Taking a trip in a car? You might need a road map. Road maps show streets and highways. Thick lines show highways. Thin lines show smaller roads.

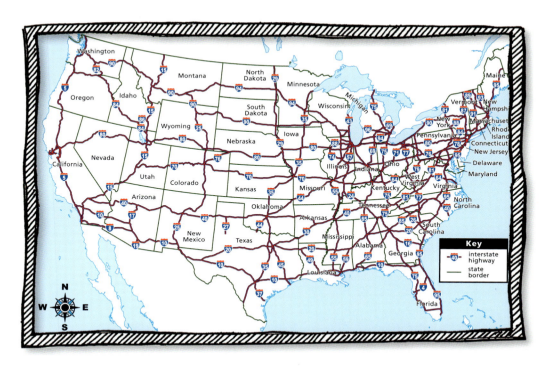

Now drivers have road maps on their phones. These digital maps tell you when to turn. They can even help if you're going the wrong way.

Other Types of Maps

Some maps teach you about people. A **population density** map shows how many people live in a place.

Athens, Greece

Greece

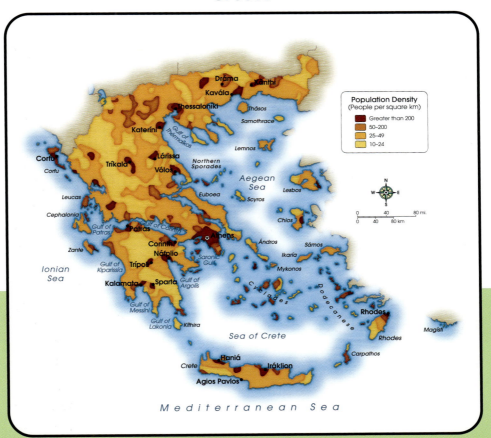

Usually, darker colors show that a lot of people live in that place. Lighter colors show that fewer people live there.

Some maps tell you about the weather. They might show the temperature in different places. They might also show that it will rain or snow in a certain place.

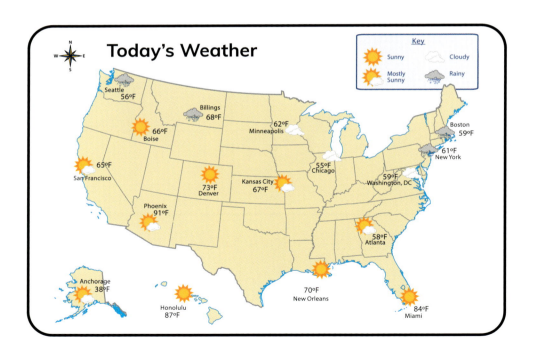

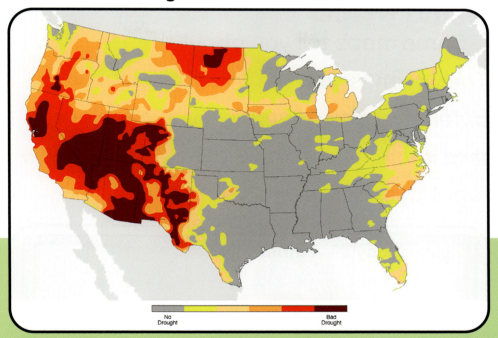

Drought in the United States

A **climate** map shows weather patterns over time. Maybe it shows how much rain falls in a year. Maybe it shows a place has had too little rain. That's called a drought.

17

Using Maps

Maps have lots of useful information. Some help you figure out where a place is. And some help get you there. Others show what to expect when you're there.

Got a question about a place? There might just be a map with the answer.

Learning from Maps

Use a political map of the United States to answer the questions below.

1. What is the capital of the United States?
2. Which states share a border with the state you live in?
3. What is one of the larger states on the map?
4. What is one of the smaller states on the map?

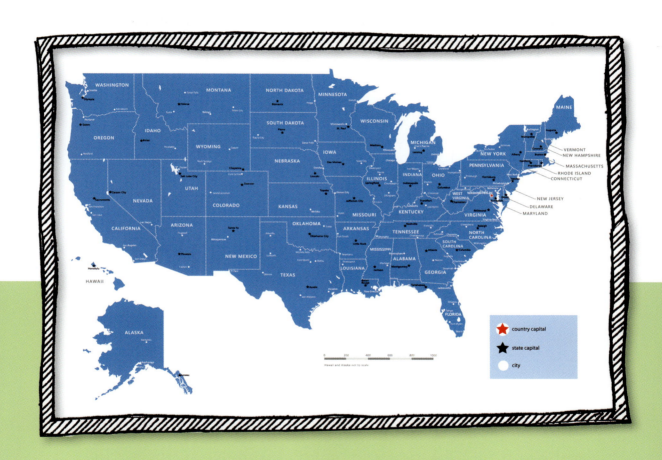

Glossary

capital (KA-puh-tuhl)—the city in a state or country where the government is based

climate (KLY-muht)—the average weather of a place throughout the year

digital (DI-juh-tuhl)—on an electronic device, like a computer or cell phone

feature (FEE-chuhr)—an important part or quality of something

globe (GLOHB)—a round model of the world

key (KEE)—a list that explains symbols

population density (pop-yuh-LAY-shuhn DEN-si-tee)—the number of people living in a certain amount of space

sphere (SFIHR)—a round, solid shape like a basketball

Read More

Adamson, Thomas K. *Landscape Maps*. Mankato, MN: Child's World, 2019.

Esbaum, Jill. *Little Kids First Big Book of Where*. Washington, DC: National Geographic Kids, 2020.

Rose, Simon. *Physical Maps*. Mankato, MN: Child's World, 2019.

Internet Sites

Generation Genius: Read About Maps
generationgenius.com/maps-of-earths-surface-reading-material

Kids Discover: Different Types of Maps
online.kidsdiscover.com/unit/geography/topic/different-types-of-maps

National Geographic Society: Map
nationalgeographic.org/encyclopedia/map/3rd-grade

Index

climate maps, 17

digital maps, 6, 13

globes, 7

keys, 9

natural features, 8

paper maps, 6

physical maps, 8–9

political maps, 10

population density maps, 14–15

road maps, 12–13

weather maps, 16

About the Author

Susan Ahmadi Hansen is a children's writer and a teacher. She especially enjoys teaching young readers and writers to fall in love with books. Susan has four adult children who live on three different continents. She lives with her husband in Cedar Park, Texas.